Seasons

Button BOOKS

ALAIN GRÉE
Seasons

The four seasons

In spring, the weather gets warmer. New plants start to grow. Summer brings hot weather. Farmers harvest their crops. In autumn, leaves fall from the trees. Winter is cold, and little grows.

spring

summer

garden in winter

garden in summer

autumn

winter

7

Spring

If you go for a walk on a spring day, what will you see? Look for the signs of spring.

Leaves grow on the trees. Birds look for twigs to build nests for their young. Flowers start to come out.

Can you see a bird in the picture? What colour is it?

Starting from seeds

The farmer uses a tractor and seed hopper to plant seeds to grow crops. But many birds like to eat the seeds. A scarecrow can scare them away. Can you stand like a scarecrow?

seed hopper

tractor

bird eating seeds

seeds

scarecrow

greenhouse

Gardeners can plant seeds in
a greenhouse. It is warm, so
seedlings soon start to grow.
The root grows out from the
bottom of the seed. Then
the shoot pops out the top.

seedling

11

The story of an apple

Have you ever looked at a cut apple? In the middle is the core. Inside are the pips. How can the pips grow into a new apple tree?

The pips in the apple are apple seeds.

Plant an apple seed in the ground and water it.

The shoot grows. It forms the stem and leaves.

The plant grows
into a tree.

In spring, pink
and white flowers
come out.

During summer,
the fruits grow.

In late summer,
they ripen into
lovely fruit.

In autumn, the
apples are ready
for picking.

Now you can eat
the tasty apples.

A new chick is born

a hen on her nest

In the spring, baby chicks are born. How does it happen? Chicks come from eggs. The mother hen lays one egg a day. When she has about ten eggs, she sits on the eggs to keep them warm until they are ready to hatch.

a chick grows inside an egg

a chick hatches

a chick is born

14

What sounds do animals make?

In the spring, mother animals call to their babies.
Can you match the animal to the sound that it makes?

duck

pig

cow

sheep

quack!

moo!

baa!

oink!

Summer

Now it is summer. It is hot and sunny. What signs of summer can you see?

Many insects fly around, and fruit grows on the trees. Summer flowers are out.

Can you see the flowers and the apple tree in the picture?

18

pressed flowers

Flowers

In the summer, it is mostly dry. We water our plants. There are lots of colourful flowers. Why not press some flowers in a heavy book? When they are dried, you can make pictures.

Insects

The forest is full of insects in the summer. How many insects can you see in the big picture? In summer, little wriggly caterpillars turn into beautiful butterflies.

caterpillar

butterfly

21

Summer fun

Summer is great for playing outdoors because it is warm. You can go camping or go for a country walk. To cool off you can swim in a pool or go to the seaside.

camping

water skiing

walking in the country

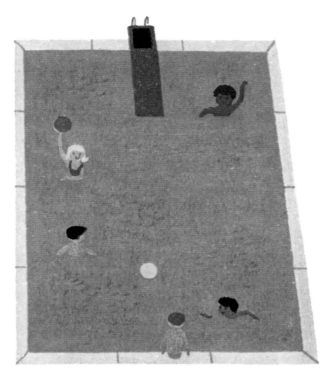

swimming

23

Keeping cool

In summer, we water the plants to stop them from drying out in the heat. We stay cool by drinking plenty of water. We can have water fights too!

Plants and people need extra water when it's hot!

watering can and hose

Summer food and drink

cold drinks

Many fruits and vegetables ripen in the summer for us to eat. Fresh fruit makes refreshing cold drinks. Which of these summer foods do you like best?

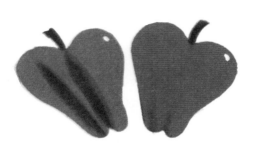

peppers

lettuce

tomatoes

ice creams and ice lolly

strawberries

cherries

watermelon

combine harvester

Harvest time

At the end of the summer, it's harvest time. The farmer uses a combine harvester to cut the crops. The grains of wheat are milled into flour. Which foods can we make with flour?

wheat sheaves

flour

wheat

blackberries

At harvest time, farmers pick fruit and vegetables. Have you ever picked blackberries? We can freeze, tin or bottle fresh fruit and vegetables to eat all year round.

green beans

apple

pear

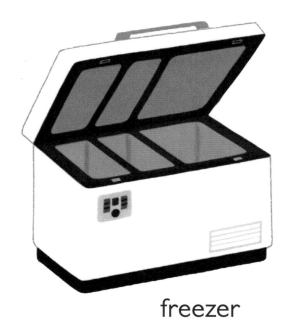

freezer

tinned fruit and vegetables

jam

bottled fruit

27

Autumn

It is autumn. The weather becomes cooler. What are the signs of autumn?

The leaves turn brown and fall off the trees. Conkers ripen and drop from the horse-chestnut trees.

There are lots of autumn flowers. What colours can you see?

a windy day

windmill

kite

Wind and rain

The autumn brings many windy days. Watch out! You might lose your hat. It's exciting to fly a kite when it's windy. The wind can be helpful. It turns the sails of windmills.

30

rain clouds

Autumn brings rain too.
Some plants and animals
love a rainy day!

snail

umbrella

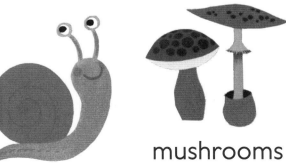
mushrooms

31

pumpkins

Autumn fun

In autumn, it's fun to gather up the old leaves to make a compost heap. The compost will help new plants to grow next year. Halloween is in autumn. Choose a pumpkin and decorate it with a scary face!

Here come some more leaves!

33

Winter is on its way

In autumn, swallows and geese fly south to warmer places. Hedgehogs, frogs and tortoises prepare to hibernate. Squirrels store nuts to eat in the winter.

swallow

goose

nuts

tortoise

frog

hedgehog

squirrel

Which of the animals can you see in the big picture?

35

Winter

It is winter. The weather is cold. Most trees and bushes have lost all their leaves. Snow lies on the ground.

Which signs of winter can you spot here? Can you see the robin? The bird's feathers keep it warm.

It's freezing!

When it is very cold, rain turns into snow and water freezes into ice. People can skate or play hockey on thick ice. How many snow and ice activities can you count?

building a snowman

sledge

ice skates

ice hockey

skiing

tobogganing

sledging

ice skating

ice curling

Winter fun

On snowy mountains, it's fun to ski. With your feet on two boards, you lean forwards to slide downhill. The poles in your hands help you balance.

Footprints in the snow

Each footprint belongs to a different animal. From the tracks, can you tell which one reaches the cosy cabin?

bird

dog

rabbit

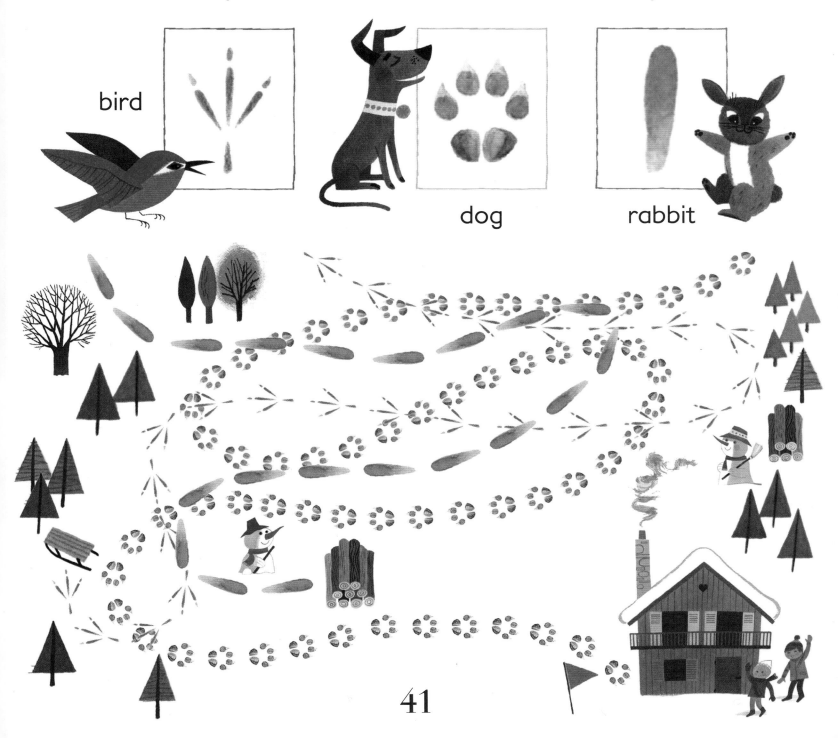

Staying warm

Farmers move animals into a barn in winter to keep them warm. They bring in straw to make the barn cosy. Which animals can you see in the barn above?

scarf

hat

socks

mittens

We wear warm clothes to play outside. After, we go back indoors to play some board games. Heaters keep us warm. It gets dark early so we turn on the lamp.

lamp

heater

Winter food and drink

It is good to have hot meals and drinks in winter to help us to stay warm. Which of these types of food do you like best?

hot drinks

potatoes

roast chicken

pasta

soup

rice

toast and butter

turnip

leeks

Santa Claus

Christmas

At Christmas Santa Claus brings presents to all the good boys and girls.

...it is warm enough to
sleep outdoors in a tent?

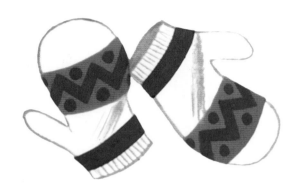

...we need to wear mittens
when we play outside?

Which season is it when...

...the swallow flies to
a warmer country?

...there are flowers
on an apple tree?

…a chick hatches
out of its egg?

…the leaves turn brown?

…Santa Claus comes?

…a caterpillar turns
into a butterfly?

ALAIN GRÉE

For more on Button Books, contact:

GMC Publications Ltd
Castle Place, 166 High Street, Lewes, East Sussex, BN7 1XU
United Kingdom
Tel +44 (0)1273 488005
www.buttonbooks.co.uk